THE BASICS OF MINISTRY SERIES

GATHER FAITHFULLY TOGETHER

GUIDE FOR SUNDAY MASS

Cardinal Roger Mahony
ARCHBISHOP OF LOS ANGELES

Feast of Our Lady of the Angels
September 4, 1997

LITURGY
TRAINING
PUBLICATIONS

Acknowledgments

The text of *Gather Faithfully Together*, copyright © 1997, Archdiocese of Los Angeles.

The English language edition of *Gather Faithfully Together* was first published on September 5, 1997, in *The Tidings*, newspaper of the Archdiocese of Los Angeles.

Guide for Sunday Mass, copyright © 1997, Archdiocese of Chicago: Liturgy Training Publications, 1800 North Hermitage Avenue, Chicago IL 60622-1101; 1-800-933-1800; fax 1-800-933-7094; e-mail orders@ltp.org. All rights reserved.

This book was edited by Gabe Huck. Audrey Novak Riley was the production editor. The design is by Anna Manhart, and the production artist was Kari Nicholls, who set the book in Goudy. Printed by Metro Litho, Chicago. The photographs on pages 9, 23, 32 and 53 are by Scott Streble. Cover photograph and all other photographs are used courtesy of *The Tidings*, newspaper of the Archdiocese of Los Angeles.

Readers of Cardinal Mahony's Pastoral Letter on the liturgy may also wish to explore Cardinal Joseph Bernardin's Pastoral Letter entitled "Our Communion, Our Peace, Our Promise." This is published by Liturgy Training Publications as *Guide for the Assembly* and includes a study and discussion guide.

Library of Congress Catalog Card number: 97-76667

ISBN 1-56854-204-6

EGMASS

01 00 99   5 4 3

CONTENTS

INTRODUCTION

1   PEACE BE WITH YOU!

2   In the early years of the Church, a bishop in Syria wrote a little instruction book for himself and other bishops. Here is one crucial task he set for bishops:

> Exhort the people to be faithful to the assembly of the Church. Let them not fail to attend, but let them gather faithfully together. Let no one deprive the Church by staying away; if they do, they deprive the Body of Christ of one of its members! (*Didascalia*, chapter 13)

3   We are centuries later, oceans apart. We are separated from that Christian Church in third-century Syria by theologies and technologies. But what we have in common surmounts all that: We the Church assemble on the Lord's Day, and that assembly, in the name of the Father and the Son and the Holy Spirit, speaks and listens to the Word of God, makes holy and is made holy by its Eucharistic praying and the sacred banquet of Holy Communion.

4   My hope is to fulfill what this bishop saw as every bishop's responsibility. As bishop of this Church of Los Angeles, I exhort you to enter into reflection with me on the Eucharist we celebrate each Sunday in our parishes.[1]

THE JUBILEE YEAR

5   Through this Letter, I want to set the direction for the way we Los Angeles Catholics approach the Jubilee Year 2000. We will have this one central work to do: to carry forward the renewal of Sunday Liturgy with vigor and joy (cf. John 16:22–24, 17:13).

6   At the start it must be clear: This will not be one task among many. It will be *the* task of these next three years. Further, I do not

see it as the narrow responsibility of the Office for Worship or the liturgy and music leaders in each parish. The tasks I set forth here are meant to unite the above persons with so many others in religious education, initiation, youth ministry, justice and outreach, and above all, the entire assembly that is this great Archdiocese and that is incarnate in the parish assemblies Sunday by Sunday.

We have been called by our Holy Father, Pope John Paul II, to make the year 2000 a Jubilee Year. Jubilee is a time to acknowledge and celebrate that things need not be what they have been, that the future need not repeat the past. Jubilee is sorting out what of that past must be forgiven or set aside, and what of the past is worthy to be grasped and handed on, built upon, made our own and given to our children. It is a time when the generation now on earth pauses, repents, gives thanks, goes forward.

THE VISION OF THE SECOND VATICAN COUNCIL

Among the finest graces of the just-ending century I would name the Second Vatican Council. Have we yet, more than 30 years after the Council, begun to absorb what the Holy Spirit did there? Have we understood the way in which that amazing gathering grappled with how the Gospel could be proclaimed and lived in the coming generations? Those of us who experienced the Council and believe it to have been such a grace to our times must ponder how broad and wise were its works, and be proud to take our tasks today from its vision.

Yes, it was a revolutionary grace, a brave moment, a Pentecost for our time. Yes, such moments are traumatic. Did the bishops of the Council know how hard renewal would be? Perhaps if they had, they would not have had the courage to begin, and to think and act in such bold ways! But they did have the courage and the vision. The prophets of this century prepare us to live in the next.

I, along with the vast majority of the People of God, stand in awe of the Council's work. I give thanks that the bishops of the

7

8

9

10

world gathered around those two great popes, John XXIII and Paul VI, and said that Gospel joy is ours and the promise of Jesus is ours; and that it is better to evangelize and love this world than to hide from, ignore, or condemn it.

11   Pope John Paul II, in calling us to the Jubilee Year, praises the Second Vatican Council and says this:

> The best preparation for the new millennium can only be expressed in a renewed commitment to apply, as faithfully as possible, the teachings of Vatican II to the life of every individual and of the whole Church. (*Tertio Millennio Adveniente: Apostolic Letter for the Jubilee of the Year 2000*, 20)

12   My hope is that we can fulfill this mandate in our Archdiocese by a singular and concentrated effort to strengthen Sunday Liturgy. Lacking that effort, we have no center, no identity as the Body of Christ. With that effort, the renewal of every aspect of our Church life becomes possible.

The renewal of the liturgy was central to the Council's vision of the Church. The Council also mandated reform and renewal because they knew that without our liturgy we will hardly know how to teach well, do justice, and love the world as God loves the world. Pope John Paul II recently spoke of how liturgy is at the heart of all our activity as the Church:

> Pastoral care will see that the liturgy is not isolated from the rest of Christian life: for the faithful are invited daily to continue their common liturgical practice in daily private prayer; this spiritual discipline gives new vigor to the witness of the faith lived by Christians each day, and also to the fraternal service of the poor and to one's neighbor in general. (Address to the French Bishops, March 8, 1997)

Oscar Romero, the late Archbishop of San Salvador, spoke in a homily of these same foundational things. Moments before his death, he talked about Eucharist as the vital center of all that the Church does. His martyrdom itself seems to be in these words:

> This holy Mass, this Eucharist, is clearly an act of faith. This body broken and blood shed for human beings encouraged us to give our body and blood up to suffering and pain, as Christ did — not for self, but to bring justice and peace to our people. (Homily, March 24, 1980)

Liturgical renewal must demonstrate how liturgy creates such Christians and such a Church, and how the ever-struggling Church makes its liturgy. Romero knew it was about life, sacrifice, and praise from the Church.

Such renewal has taken us many years, with numerous successes and some problems. So difficult have been these first efforts that some seem ready to declare it a failure, an embarrassing mistake of Vatican II. Others would say we have come as far as was intended, so let us hear no more of liturgical renewal. And yet others call this task meaningless in light of the great need for the Church to throw itself into causes of justice and peace.

13

14

15

16

17   Yet it seems to me that only now are we getting glimpses of that wondrous experience when a parish lives by that full, conscious and active participation in the liturgy by all the faithful. The situation is unfortunately uneven. Only in some parishes have we seen the sustained effort from well-prepared leaders to work over many years toward a Sunday Liturgy that is for the people of that parish the nourishment they need, the deeds of Word and Eucharist they cherish. But there are beginnings here, and these cause us both to rejoice and to focus on what can be learned.

START WITH SUNDAY EUCHARIST

18   The Jubilee Year calls out to us to take those gifts the Spirit raised up in the Church at Vatican II. Take them with the wisdom gained these last three decades. Come into the new Millennium doing Gospel deeds throughout all realms of human life because a compelling and contemplative celebrating of Eucharist is our doing and God's, Sunday after Sunday.

19   At the head of our calendar stands Sunday, still called by us the Lord's Day, the First Day of creation, the Day when Christ defeated death and the Spirit blew upon the disciples. (*Catechism of the Catholic Church* [hereafter, CCC], 2174–2175) It is above all the day when we assemble. Saint Justin tried to explain to the non-Christians in Rome what Christians were all about:

> On the day called Sunday there is a meeting in one place of those who live in cities or the country, and the memoirs of the apostles or the writing of the prophets are read as long as time permits. Then we all stand up together and offer prayers. And when we have finished the prayer, bread is brought, and wine and water, and the president similarly sends up prayers and thanksgivings to the best of his ability, and the congregation assents, saying the Amen; the distribution and reception of the consecrated elements by each one takes place and they are sent to the absent by the deacons. . . . We all hold this common gathering on Sunday, since it is the first day, on which God transforming darkness and matter made the universe,

and Jesus Christ our Savior rose from the dead on the same day. (*Apology*, second century, 67:3 – 5, 7)

To celebrate Sunday Eucharist the followers of Jesus risked their lives in some times and places. Such was the gathering, such was the praise of God given there, such was the need to assemble the Church and make the Eucharist! In our day, the obstacles are perhaps greater than hostile emperors. What will it take to reclaim this day and its holiness? None of us know that, but we know that we do not live without our Lord's Day and its assembly.[2] The vigor of that assembly, its beauty and its liveliness, its quiet and its passion, are what I want to address in this Letter.   20

I will focus on the Sunday Eucharist, but I do so knowing that the ritual life of the Church does and must extend far beyond that gathering on the Lord's Day. I will focus on what we need to do in these next few years. I must recognize at the start what the Council itself recognized in paragraph 14 of the *Constitution on the Sacred Liturgy*. This immense renewal of the liturgy of the Church can be done only when those who are primarily responsible for the parish liturgy are themselves persons "imbued with the spirit of the liturgy."   21

I believe this to be true, but I also recognize that the summons to renewal came because liturgical practice in the Church had, in many ways, ceased to be a source for such rich formation. The condition, "imbued with the spirit of the liturgy," was realistic, but it was far easier said than done. Where was the liturgical practice that would form such pastors in the spirit of the liturgy? It was a long task the Council set in motion and much of it rests now, as it did then, in the hands of those pastors. How are they to be formed by the liturgy and so live from it and lead their parishes toward a vital, joyous liturgy?   22

The second part of this Letter is addressed to priests and to all others who bear leadership responsibility for the liturgy. We have learned in these years since Vatican II that the renewal of parish liturgy does not happen without the support, hard work, and constant learning and evaluation by those who preside — the priests of   23 the Archdiocese. They are not the only ones responsible, but they are essential. With thanks for all they have done and are doing, I invite them to join me in this entire reflection and active renewal.

TENSIONS

24 The obstacles to such a renewal of our parish Sunday Liturgy could paralyze us, could keep us from even beginning. I want to name some of these and discuss one of them. I would like to see them as challenges that keep us attentive and honest in this work, as creative tensions that call forth creative responses.

Solemnity and Community

25 Liturgy calls forth reverence. The beauty of its aesthetics, its signs of solemnity and choreography of ministries, its poetry and its silences, lift us in awe before the mystery of God. Yet, liturgy is to be festive. It is about the communion and radical equality of the Baptized, their union in the Lord, their friendly sharing of ministry and life. It builds community by breaking open the meaning of God's Word for our everyday lives, and by gathering us as a family around the Lord's Table. We do not choose between solemnity and festivity, between reverence and community. The vertical and the horizontal dimensions of liturgy must be held together to work for us.

External Form and Internal Transformation

26 The external form of liturgy is a communication. It teaches and forms the assembly. The order of actions and the use of symbols challenge and invite us into the truths of the faith and the spiritual Tradition we have received. Yet, liturgy is alive. It must have flesh and blood and spirit. It flows from our deep conversion to the Lord and the joy of knowing him. It must speak to this people, here and now. We do not need mere mechanical implementation in response to liturgical directives any more than we need a liturgy that seems to be of the presider's own making. We need a faithfulness to the official directives and common forms, but a faithfulness that is

imbued with the Spirit, and that opens this Sunday assembly to the riches of Eucharistic faith.

Unity and Diversity

We are one. Our Catholic faith will not allow the distinction "us" versus "them." On Sunday we gather in one Lord, one faith, one Baptism. Yet, we are many. When we gather, it is also to witness to the universality of our faith, evident in the many parts that make up the one Body. We celebrate the diverse experiences, cultures, and charisms that assemble around the one table. Because of the uniqueness of our local Church in this regard, we must say more.

27

THE CHALLENGE AND BLESSING OF MANY CULTURES

The liturgy not only can but must build on what is suitable in the culture of a people. In our Archdiocese we Catholics come from

28

many cultures with many different gifts. The Lord has brought us all together and we are called to be fully Christ together. In population, we are predominately from Spanish-speaking cultures, with all their own diversity. But we embrace many Asian and Pacific Island cultures as well as the diversity of various African and European cultures that have had their own development on this continent. And there is cultural richness within cultural richness.

29   This is a difficult challenge. Yes, we want liturgy with sounds and gestures that flow from the religious soul of a people, whether Vietnamese or Mexican, Native American or African American. Yet we have a Catholic soul. We are in need of witnessing to that soul, of being in assemblies where the vision of Paul comes alive, where the Vietnamese, the Mexican, Native American and African American stand side by side around the table singing one thanksgiving to God. And although that thanksgiving may have the rhythm of one particular culture, all will join with their hearts. Before we are anything else — any sex, ethnicity, nationality or citizenship — we need to be the Body of Christ, sisters and brothers by our Baptism. Every one of us needs to know by heart some of the music, vocabulary, movement, and ways of thinking and feeling that are not of our own background. The larger society we are a part of needs this witness.

30   We have to accomplish two results: to let the prevalent liturgy take on the pace, sounds, and shape that other cultures bring; and to strive in our parishes to witness that in this Church there is finally no longer this people or that people, but one single assembly in Christ Jesus. (CCC: 1207)

31   Either task would be difficult; together they seem daunting. We can be discouraged and do neither, or we can be excited by the challenge. But imagine liturgies where the economic and racial segregations of our society are overcome. The language of Pentecost, many languages speaking God's praise at the same time, is our language and our heritage. It goes far beyond vocabulary. It is God made manifest in the gifts of every people. (CCC: 1204)

Catholics speak this Pentecost language. This is no melting | 32
pot. This is communion. Communion means life together. Communion means we share and share alike, yet each person comes to that Communion in the full stature of his or her culture.

This striving for catholicity extends beyond ethnicity: The | 33
Sunday assembly should bring together men, women and children of all ages. It should be the one experience in our lives when we will not be sorted out by education level, skin color, intelligence, politics, sexual orientation, wealth or lack of it, or any other human condition. If the assembly is the basic symbol when the liturgy is celebrated (CCC: 1188), the comfortable homogeneity promoted by so many in this nation has no place. Homogeneity and comfort are not Gospel values.

I want to warn against an excessive "inculturation" that is | 34
destroying our liturgy. In the past generation, we have introduced into the liturgy some practices and attitudes from North American society that have no place there. For example: the hurried pace, the tyranny of the clock, the inattention to the arts, the casual tone of a presider, the "what can I get out of it?" approach of the consumer, the "entertain me" attitude of a nation of television watchers. All these are the wrong sort of inculturation. Their prevalence shows how difficult it is to seek what in the culture offers a true correspondence with the spirit of the liturgy.

I hope that what follows — Part One addressed to all, Part | 35
Two addressed primarily to those responsible for the parish liturgy week by week — will be read in light of this tension. We have obligations: to explore inculturation in our many ethnic traditions, to strive for a broad catholicity in the makeup of our parishes, and to be critical of those ways in which the mainstream culture has at times deformed the liturgy and robbed it of its power.

AN INVITATION

All this sounds difficult, but I believe there is a starting point: | 36
Sunday Mass. That is what the remainder of this Letter speaks

about. From these years of experience with the renewal of the liturgy, we know many practices and principles that can be applied now, in all our parishes, to the worthy celebration of Sunday Mass. That application is to be our work, even if other work must be put aside over these years that take us to the Jubilee Year. What we accomplish together will shape the Church of our Archdiocese in the new Millennium. With much catechesis and preparation in our parishes, what we will have in place by the year 2000 will grow stronger and deeper in the first decade of the new Millennium.

37   During these next years we will begin using the second English edition of the Sacramentary and the Revised New American Bible Lectionary. The renewal of Sunday Liturgy suggested in this Letter will be excellent preparation for introducing the revised Sacramentary.

38   Liturgical renewal is a matter of passion, of catching some glimpse of the way strong Sunday Liturgy makes strong Catholics, and of how these Catholics make their Sunday Liturgy. (CCC: 1324) That, I believe, is the insight and the determination needed, whatever the ethnic composition of the parish. It is good news.

PART ONE

A MESSAGE TO ALL CATHOLICS
OF THE ARCHDIOCESE OF LOS ANGELES

SUNDAY MASS, 2000

I am going to share with you my vision of a parish Sunday
Eucharist. It is a summer Sunday in the Jubilee Year 2000, 30 minutes before the 10 A.M. Mass at Our Lady of the Angels parish.
Already, several members of the choir are talking together and trying bits of music with the director and the cantor. Soon the first
usher to arrive is tidying up the entrance way and removing any
bulletins left in the assembly's area at the last Mass. The sacristan
has placed the bread and wine on a covered table near the
entrance.[3] Servers, lectors and communion ministers begin to arrive
and go about their necessary preparations. By now the early comers
are here, some kneeling in prayer or sitting quietly. Others stop in
the Blessed Sacrament chapel; others light candles in the alcove
that holds an image of Our Lady of Guadalupe. As 10 o'clock nears,
more people stop to write in the parish's Book of Intercessions.

39

The Entrance of the Assembly

In houses and apartments all through the neighborhood, the true
entrance procession of this Mass has been in full swing, sometimes
calm, sometimes hectic. Sunday clothes are being put on. Many
families are finishing breakfast, conscious of the one-hour fast. Here
and there are adults who choose to fast altogether until taking Holy
Communion. Some households make a conscious effort to keep the

40

morning quiet: no radio or television, and the Sunday papers wait until later in the day.

41   In a surprisingly large number of households, but still a tiny minority, the Sunday Scriptures have already been read aloud together on Friday or Saturday evening. Others met during the week in Spanish-speaking or English-speaking prayer groups where the Lectionary's Sunday readings were pondered. Teenagers spent part of the regular youth group meeting reading these Scriptures.

42   When we think about preparing for liturgy, we usually think of the ministers — the choir rehearsing, the lectors engaging their readings all through the week, the homilist spending some time every day of the week until it all comes together on Saturday, those who care for the sacred space keeping it clean and beautiful. But the liturgy is the work of the whole assembly, and here we begin to see that many take this seriously. Many have prepared themselves to come together today and participate fully in this Eucharist.

43   So this is the entrance procession, coming from all directions, made up of all ages, several races, a variety of economic circumstances and political outlooks — and speaking at least three first languages! But they are all in a great procession, the Church assembling in the house of the Church. "We shall go up with joy," "Que alegría cuando me dijeron vamos a la casa del Señor," or as we used to pray from Psalm 43, "Introibo ad altare Dei." On the way to that altar of God, most of these people pass by the large Baptismal Font and take water from it, perhaps remembering their own Baptism. They enter their liturgy marked with the water of Baptism, marked with the cross of Christ whose Body we became in those waters. (CCC: 1267)

44   At 9:45 the choir is assembled and a brief but serious rehearsal begins, firming up what was practiced last Wednesday evening. This warm-up of voices lasts until just a few minutes before the liturgy is to begin; toward the end many in the now two-thirds full church join in singing. By now the presider is vested and stands with servers and lectors near the main entrance, adding to the welcome of the ushers. The ushers, knowing the church will be full, are doing their

best to fill the pews nearest the altar first. They make special efforts to see that parents with very small infants get places in the first rows (where there are more comfortable chairs).

Likewise, the ushers invite any who would find the commu-   45
nion procession difficult to take places in those areas throughout the assembly space with room for wheelchairs. The ushers point out to any newcomers with pre-school children that child care is avail- able, or they are welcome to have their children with them (it is surely not appropriate to have them in a separate room). The sac- ristan has invited the gift-bearers to bring the bread and wine for- ward at the proper time and is now going over the "checklist for Sunday Mass" before joining the assembly. Sponsors and catechu- mens find each other and fill in the first few rows of one section of the church.

Although people go out of their way to greet one another and   46
be gracious, it is never done in such a way that you feel one person is the host and another is the guest. Everyone is at home.

47   At one minute before 10 o'clock, the cantor greets the assembly and asks them to give some brief attention to the hymn that will be used as a recessional today. As they conclude this little rehearsal, the cantor announces the hymnal number of the procession song, then stands quietly for a moment before gesturing for everyone to rise as the instrumentalists begin to lead everyone into singing a hymn of praise that seems to build verse by verse. The procession of servers with cross and candles, lectors (one of them with the Lectionary held high), and presider waits at the edge of the assembly until the second verse begins, then moves slowly forward. By that time, each minister, including the presider, is singing.

48   At Our Lady of the Angels, the renovation put people on three sides of the area where the altar and the ambo are, so most members of the assembly are able to participate more fully with the other members of the assembly. For a year now it has been the custom, once the entrance song begins, for the people on either side of the aisle in the long central part of the church to turn toward the aisle until the procession has passed. In fact, they are turning toward each other, becoming conscious of each other's presence as the church begins its liturgy. The peace greeting, when it comes later on, will somehow seal this communion, this sense of being not individuals, but the assembled Church offering its praise, thanks, lament and intercession before God.

49   As the singing continues, the presider greets the altar with a kiss. At the chair, he continues to sing with the assembly. When the singing ends, all make the Sign of the Cross: We do all that we do in the name of Father, Son and Holy Spirit. Looking at the assembly, the presider then exchanges the greeting. In two or three well-prepared sentences he invites — maybe exhorts is a better word — the assembly to enter well into this liturgy. He is careful not to speak in any way that would imply it is his liturgy, or that the people assembled are guests. Nothing he says makes trivial what is about to be done here.

50   The rites by which the community assembles are quite simple during these Sundays in Ordinary Time compared with how the

parish begins its liturgy during the seasons of Advent and Christmas, Lent and Easter. Year-round, however, these rites conclude when the presider calls everyone to prayer: "Oremos/Let us pray." And then, in response, silence. This silence is long enough to settle into, and like song, creates the Church. The presider has been praying this opening prayer all week by himself, and now he speaks it in a clear and understandable proclamation. The loud "Amen" says that the assembly has heard.

When the people at Our Lady of the Angels sit down, there is usually a sense that in all these moments—from the alarm clock to this Amen—the Spirit has brought them somewhere: into the worship space they call the "church," and even more into the Church itself, into the assembly that will here pray not as so many individuals, but as the Body of Christ. 51

The Liturgy of the Word

All the readers of Scripture know what they are there to do. They know that these readings could be read privately by each individual, but that this public reading is quite different. For two years now there have been no booklets for the assembly to follow the reading, although by the front doors there are Sunday Missals for the hearing-impaired and for those whose language is different from the one used at this Mass. The assembly gives all its attention to the lector. 52

These lectors have been struggling with the assigned Scripture for the past few days. Their manner and understanding may vary, but they open this Lectionary and read *knowing that this* church is full of people hungry for the Word of God. 53

The lectors have taken the time to hear anew old words, to let the images of Scripture reflect against and mingle with their lives. Each has found something to cherish in a reading, something to be passionate about. But they also know how to communicate their passion without calling attention to themselves. The assembly is hearing God's Word. You can tell that the main activity going on during these readings is good listening. And what a treasure that is! The liturgy—God's word proclaimed and God's word listened to 54

— is being carried by the assembly and they mean it when they say, "Thanks be to God/Demos gracias a Dios." Every Sunday the Sacred Scriptures have been opened and read aloud. God's Word proclaimed and listened to will be the foundation for all else that this Church does. (Lectionary, Introduction, 1, 10; or *General Instruction of the Roman Missal*, 8)

55   Silence follows the first and second readings at Our Lady of the Angels, and again after the homily, lasting about a minute. People are used to it, and know what to do with it. They will tell you: Let that reading echo in your head, cling to a word or a phrase, savor it, stand under it. It becomes a very still time. Babies fuss, but people are not distracted.

56   The psalm after the first reading is almost an extension of this silence. No one gets out a book because the parish uses a repertoire of perhaps a dozen psalms — and each year they learn one or two more — where all can sing the refrain by heart. The cantor at this Mass, like the other cantors at Our Lady of the Angels, knows that people want to hear the words. Good articulation is as important

as a good voice. Sometimes the homilists bring the psalm, and especially the refrain, into the homily. Sometimes the texts appear in the parish bulletin with the suggestion that these psalms be prayed at home. In these ways and more (seasonal evening prayer, for example), the people of Our Lady of the Angels are coming to know the Church's oldest prayer book, the Psalter.

Another reader comes forward for the second Scripture and again silence follows. There is nothing half-hearted about the procession that now begins: The alleluia is singing to move with, to process with; it takes candle-bearing servers, incense bearer, and book-bearing presider through the assembly and to the place of proclamation. 57

A regular churchgoer usually knows within a sentence or two whether the homilist worked hard enough on the homily. This Sunday and every Sunday at Our Lady of the Angels, the expectation is that not only did the preacher work on this homily, but so did the ten or so people who meet every week on, say, Monday evenings to read, pray with and talk about the Scriptures for the coming weeks. The homilists are committed to being there and lectors often come as well. Sometimes these Monday night meetings give yesterday's homily a review. Noticeable progress has been made since this practice began, although some weeks are better than others. Two years ago the parish staff, parish council and homilists made a pact: Homilists would give adequate time to preparing the homily (including the Monday night meeting), and the staff and council would find ways to assume other parish and pastoral duties and responsibilities, thus freeing up the priests. 58

Something else is evident this morning: The habit of listening calls forth a preacher's best. And this assembly knows how to listen. 59

> Listening is not an isolated moment. It is a way of life. It means openness to the Lord's voice not only in the Scriptures but in the events of our daily lives and in the experience of our brothers and sisters. It is not just my listening but our listening together for the Lord's word to the community. (*Fulfilled in Your Hearing*, 20)

60   Although there is no set time for a homily's length, about ten to twelve minutes on this Sunday in Ordinary Time seems best for both homilists and listeners. And the homilists know it takes time to prepare a well-focused ten- to twelve-minute homily.

61   After a minute or so of silence, after the homily, five catechumens (who hope to be called to Baptism next Easter) and seven candidates (who on Easter will be welcomed into full communion) are dismissed to continue studying the Scriptures. Two catechists go with them. The assembly sees these people week after week for a year or more. They are very much a part of this parish community.

62   The Creed is a loud, almost mighty sound, chant-like. Few need the text as the rhythm carries it along. Then the Liturgy of the Word comes to its conclusion in prayerful intercession. No longer is there a dull reading of bland texts with a weak "Lord, hear our prayer/Te lo pedimos Señor" after each. Today the cantor chants the intercessions. The texts are short and strong. Only a few are written new each week, and these echo some image or notion from the day's Scriptures and the week's news. The assembly is engaged in this rhythmic exchange with the cantor. One would have to believe that these people regularly pray in their homes for the world and the Church, for the sick and the dead. The back and forth of cantor and assembly shows that this parish is standing together before the Lord and demanding to be heard.

The Liturgy of the Eucharist

63 Everyone sits down to recollect themselves and to focus their attention on the table of the Lord, which is now reverently prepared with the plate of bread, the cup and a large flagon of wine. Nothing distracts from the power of the bread and wine in their simple vessels. Last Sunday the choir sang, but today all keep silent as the table is prepared. Ushers pass baskets. More than once over the past years the homilists have talked about almsgiving in the Catholic tradition, for both the Church and the poor. These have been homilies, not "money talks," when the Scriptures or something else in the day's liturgy suggested that the assembly consider

its mission, its responsibilities, and what it means to trust God. The parish bulletin regularly prints financial information to support both aspects of the parish's mission, caring for the poor and for the Church. Writing a check or coming up with cash is a vital liturgical deed in the root meaning of liturgy, a work done by people on behalf of the larger community. (CCC: 1070)

Selected members of the assembly then bring the gifts of the assembly in procession to the presider who receives them in thanksgiving as the personal sacrificial offerings of the people of God. (CCC: 1350, 1351)

After the Prayer over the Gifts, the Eucharistic Prayer begins. Here we are at the center of Catholic praying and that center is Eucharistic. The presider gives the ancient summons to "lift up your hearts" and to give the Lord praise and thanks. The dialogue is chanted — strongly, loudly, and back and forth to make clear that what is about to happen needs the full and active participation of everyone. The presider's posture and gestures invoke such participation, the way his voice does in dialogue and proclamation.

This participation in the Eucharistic Prayer has been the greatest change at Our Lady of the Angels. The parish always worked for good singing and good lectors. But the Eucharistic Prayer was a kind of orphan. People said, "We lift them up to the Lord," and sang the "Holy, Holy." But for years no one could have told you anything about the Eucharistic Prayer except that "the priest does the consecration." Now the parishioners can talk about the experience of standing and singing God's praise together; they can see how much their lives need to be filled with thanksgiving; and they recognize that their presence to one another at this table witnesses to the breadth of the Church in place and in time, a holy communion. They can talk about solidarity with one another across all dividing lines. They can talk about sacrifice and the mystery of Christ's passion, death and resurrection that is remembered and realized here in a powerful shaping of their own lives. Above all, they can talk about the way the Holy Spirit is invoked to transform these gifts and themselves. And so they are talking about the

64

65

66

presence of Christ in the simple gifts of bread and wine, and in the mystery that is this Church. (CCC: 1352–1354)

67 Great mystery is conveyed in the faces and postures, singing and silence, gesture and word. Everyone is attentive, bodies engaged as much as hearts. It is clearly the central moment of this Lord's Day gathering. Over the altar and the gifts of bread and wine, all God's saving deeds are remembered, all is held up in praise of God, all is asked of God. The Catholic sensibility to sacrament, to the presence of God, is never more joyous, never more challenging. We need to take care in our thinking and in our language: When we say "Eucharist," we mean this whole action of presider and assembly. That is the Eucharist whose grace and powerful mystery can transform us and, in us, the world. (CCC: 1368)

68 The presider chants most of the Prayer and the refrains are the same most Sundays of the year, sung to music capable of carrying the liturgy week after week. The exchange between presider and assembly is seamless, as proclamation and acclamation are woven together. The Prayer takes only four or five minutes, but in its intensity it is clearly the center of this Sunday gathering. As was said long ago, the Church makes the Eucharist and the Eucharist makes the Church. And that is what we take part in on a Sunday morning. No wonder that when the great "Amen" is concluded, one can sense a collective sigh, a deep breath.

69 The chanting of the Our Father then carries the assembly toward Holy Communion. The peace greeting is not long or protracted, but it is anything but perfunctory. People seem to look each other in the eye. They clasp hands firmly or embrace. As the presider raises a large piece of the consecrated bread to break it, the cantor begins the litany "Lamb of God/Cordero de Dios" that will carry us until the bread is all broken, the consecrated wine all poured into the communion cups, "God's holy gifts for God's holy people."

70 Holy Communion is a procession at Our Lady of the Angels, a practice parishioners have worked hard to bring about. Two years ago, row by row, from the front to the back, people lined up for

Communion. During Eastertime the homilists talked — and after Mass so did many people — about what the Communion time means. The key was unfolding the wonder and thanksgiving Catholics feel toward the Body of Christ — the consecrated bread and wine, and the Church. Both have the same name. What does it mean when the Body of Christ comes forward to receive the Body of Christ? The sense of a Church in procession has somehow replaced the feeling of individuals lining up. For example, the first to come forward are no longer those in the front pew; rather, the people in the back pews begin the procession so that the whole room seems to be surrounded by a procession of people. Here is a Church partaking of the sacred banquet.

The invitation to Communion, "This is the Lamb of God," and the assembly's response are followed immediately by the beginning of the Communion procession song. At this point, the procession is moving — that is, the ministers of Communion are at the Communion stations beginning the Communion of the assembly.

71

72   The ordinary and extraordinary ministers of the Eucharist this Sunday represent the diversity of the community: women and men, young and old, of different races, backgrounds and circumstances. They are in no hurry and neither is the assembly. Yet there seem to be enough of them that the procession can keep moving while each individual is treated with reverence: Ministers look each person in the eye and say, without rushing, "The Body of Christ/El Cuerpo de Cristo," "The Blood of Christ/La Sangre de Cristo." Each person has time to respond, "Amen." The ministers, also without hurrying, then place the Body of Christ in the hand or on the tongue, and give over the Blood of Christ.

73   The song that is sung throughout is good for processing: No one needs to carry the printed words because only six or seven songs are used at communion throughout the year. They fit the movement and the moment. Each is sung often enough to be familiar, and each has a melody and words that flourish with repetition. This Sunday's single Communion song continues until presider and assembly sit down after all have taken Holy Communion.

74   It took some years before most of the assembly received the Blood of Christ as well as the Body of Christ. Perhaps the spirit of invitation did it, a spirit that recognizes how this drink from the cup of consecrated wine is needed by each of us in our thirst, how this drinking complements the eating of the consecrated bread. Eventually the assembly began to hear the simple words: "Take this, all of you, and drink from it. . . ."

75   Perhaps because the assembly at Our Lady of the Angels has clearly discovered how to make the Eucharistic Prayer so conscious and intense, the whole of their Communion Rite is compelling—from the Lord's Prayer to the silent and still time after all have received. People are intent on the hard work of liturgy, caught up in singing, procession and even silence. To be with them is to know deeply that we are the Body and Blood of Christ. To be with them is to learn how to be in this world with reverence, with a love of God that is incarnate in how we speak to others, how we move amidst the holiness of matter and of time.

We must capture again the great power of silence within our
Sunday Liturgies. Too often the impression has been given that
properly celebrated liturgy must be filled with sounds: prayer, song,
speech — regarding silence as a vacuum to be avoided at all costs.
But we have come to learn that we all need the gift of silence
throughout liturgy in order to help us enter more fully and deeply
into the mystery of the death and resurrection of the Lord Jesus.
The silence and the stillness in the church become a wondrous
mixture of personal and communal prayer.

Above all, Our Lady of the Angels has learned that the steady
experience of a participatory ritual can carry the Church Sunday to
Sunday. People do not want to be entertained and passive. They
want to become energized in the hard but delightful work of liturgy,
praising and thanking God, remembering the liberating deeds of
God, interceding for all the world. These desires are most clear
when people enter into the spirit of the Eucharistic Prayer and
share in the Paschal Banquet. What a witness to the Spirit-inspired
work of Vatican II!

Taking Leave

At Our Lady of the Angels this Sunday the announcements are a
transition from the final quiet and peace of the Communion to the
sending forth. The various activities of the week are announced,
then all stand and the presider prays the blessing and the dismissal.
A concluding song leads to much visiting and to the procession out.
I mean the true procession of this Church: one, two, and five at a
time going back to neighborhoods and homes, roles and jobs, studies and waiting. But Sunday by Sunday the world is here being
transformed in Christ!

Visiting Our Lady of the Angels Parish

I have tried to describe what makes Our Lady of the Angels parish
breathe and exercise its life in Christ. The description had to be
detailed to give the whole content. I have not outlined how I want
liturgy to look in every parish of our Archdiocese three years from

76

77

78

79

now. Look first for the texture. The details are important because care for details matters greatly in liturgy, but these are the details of Our Lady of the Angels. The details at your parish will differ — but each parish should intend to have this beauty and intensity each Sunday.

FROM HERE TO THERE

80   "How could I survive without Sunday Mass in my parish? I have to be there with my parish on Sundays. I am needed!" That must be what Sunday obligation is about for us, and that is what I hope Catholic life can be like as we urgently process in this renewal.

81   I want to kindle a passion for a vital Sunday Liturgy in every parish of our Archdiocese. And I will support the various ways to do that by taking responsibility for providing training and supporting leadership. Enthusiasm for this work, a blessing of the Holy Spirit, must be immense.

I will, both personally and through the agencies of the Archdiocese, ensure that the priests and others who are responsible for the parish liturgy receive what they need to lead toward such vital liturgy. 82

But one thing must come from you, the people of the parishes. Please give every kind of encouragement to your priests to use the opportunities we provide for formation in liturgy. Priests must know that the people of their parishes believe that this is time and money well spent, and that their parishioners want the following which can only come from their pastors: 83

• **Better presiding:** How can priests be better in their role at the Sunday liturgy?

• **Better preaching:** How can priests improve the content and the delivery of the homily on Sunday?

• **Better leadership:** How can priests themselves be leaders and work confidently with other parish leaders in bringing the whole parish toward the kind of Sunday Liturgy I have described?

The first two are specific, and we will provide ongoing help of various kinds in both areas. 84

The third, however, is what we have lacked, yet it is a most critical factor in a deeply rooted renewal of the liturgy. Better leadership would include the following: 85

• teaching about the liturgy;

• preaching that takes seriously the assembly's experience of the liturgy and builds up that experience; and

• above all, seeking in the liturgy one's deeply Catholic spirituality and the very shape of a Catholic life.

I ask you to support your priests as we focus on such matters in these next few years. This becomes more complex when we face the decreasing number of ordained priests and the number of parishes that have up to a dozen Sunday Masses in overcrowded spaces. There are no simple solutions, but these circumstances cannot be a reason to delay the renewal of the liturgy. In many 86 parishes a first step would be a staff position for a parish liturgy director. Approaching this goal by clustering or twinning parishes might be more effective. Such a staff position should not further segregate the various parish activities (school, religious education, outreach), but can be the occasion for a breakthrough in cooperation and understanding of how the liturgy is the concern and the life of the entire staff.

87   As formation of the clergy toward better presiding, preaching and leadership takes place, you will be challenged to do what only you, the Baptized members of the parish, can and must do if we are to fulfill the vision of Vatican II. I would ask you to think of your own involvement in the following ways:

1. Your right, your duty

88   Come on Sunday knowing your dignity: In Baptism, you put on Christ. You are the Body of Christ. Vatican II, in the *Constitution on the Sacred Liturgy*, said that "full, conscious and active participation by all the faithful" was the "right and the duty" of all the faithful *because of their Baptism* (14).

89   It has taken more than three decades for those profound insights to take hold. Most of us were satisfied to look for something less than what was intended: We were happy when a parish had good singing, and when lector and Communion ministries were done well.

90   But good singing and good ministry are not enough. You who are baptized have duties that are wrapped up in that kind of participation the Council called "full," "conscious" and "active." When we consider the Sunday Liturgy at Our Lady of the Angels in 2000, we can form some working notions of each of those qualities.

91   "Full" participation brings us to the liturgy, body and soul, with all our might. It begins long before the liturgy in making sure that Sunday Mass is not just one more thing on our "must do" list. The people of Our Lady of the Angels let the time of liturgy be first. They do not just keep the time of Mass from disruptions; they give it room in their lives. They have some good habits: perhaps looking

over the Scriptures, or fasting until Mass, or not distracting themselves in the early hours of Sunday. They come to Mass mindful of their responsibility — to themselves, one another, and God. Because they want the priest, choir and lector to prepare, they know that they too must prepare to be good members of the assembly.

"Full" participation also means that a baptized person does not mentally weave in and out of the liturgy. Our duty is not just to be present; our duty is to be fully present. The songs are for singing, the Scriptures for listening, the silence for reflecting, the intercessions for pleading, the Eucharistic Prayer for immense thanksgiving, the Communion for every kind of hunger and thirst satisfied in partaking together of the Body and Blood of Christ, and the dismissal for going out to love the world the way God does. 92

In addition, our participation is to be "conscious." We must enter with great openness into the chant and song, the processions and gestures, the words and silences of the liturgy. "Conscious" participation is opening every part of ourselves — body, mind and spirit — to what we do at the liturgy. We stand consciously and with attention. If we reach out our hands to the Body and Blood of Christ, we do so with grace, mindful of our hunger and the world's hunger, and of God's goodness. 93

Another way to be "conscious" at the liturgy is to be aware of our Baptism. We come on the Lord's Day to the table of the Eucharist because we have been through the waters of Baptism. Because we died to our old selves and became alive in Christ, we gather on Sunday, not as isolated persons, but as the Church, with its diversity of cultures, languages, and races. This is difficult for those accustomed to think of themselves as autonomous individuals — workers, taxpayers, citizens. But here, the liturgy is celebrated by the assembled Church. 94

Cultivate, then, your deep awareness that it is not so many individuals who are standing here singing, but the Church. It is not individuals who are coming forward to the table, but the Church. It is not even individuals who are going forth to live by the Word they have listened to and the Body and Blood of Christ they have eaten and tasted. It is the Church going forth as a leaven in the midst of 95 the world God loves. This is perhaps the most difficult part of the whole renewal.

96 "Active" is the third quality of the Baptized person's participation. Please do not see "active" as the opposite of "contemplative." Some of our activity at liturgy is contemplation. Part of the genius of the Roman Rite is that it presumes a beauty on which our spirits can feast. If we have too often seen "active" as "busy," consider the liturgy at Our Lady of the Angels and see the wealth of silence, as well as the powerful reading of Scripture, and preaching and singing of psalms to engage our contemplation.

97 "Active" participation also calls us to attend to others, to a kind of presence. This is crucial to what Catholic liturgy is all about. Such attention to others has at least two manifestations.

98 First, we are here not to make our own prayer while each other person in the church at the same time makes his or her own prayer. We are Baptized people standing with other Baptized people. Our thanksgiving is in the Church's thanksgiving. Our attention to God's Word is in the assembly's attention. Our intercession is in the Church's intercession. The mystery of our transfiguration in Christ is in the whole body of Baptized people transfigured. (CCC: 1136–1141)

99 To create solidarity, be attentive to where you take your place and set a good example. Go as close as possible to the Eucharistic table. Go to the middle of the pew and sit next to somebody and make room for others next to you. The Body of Christ has to be visible, audible, tangible. Pope John Paul II recently called for bishops to attend to the quality of the signs by which the liturgy takes place, and he stressed that "the first sign is that of the assembly itself . . . Everyone's attitude counts, for the liturgical assembly is the first image the church gives" (Address to the French Bishops, March 8, 1997).

100 Second, "active" participation means the awareness that at liturgy, we never close out the larger world. The liturgy shows us Gospel living and how to be in the world. Catholic morality, how we deal in justice and charity day by day with great and small

matters, is to be encountered and uncovered from our active participation in the liturgy.

2. Ministries

The liturgy at Our Lady of the Angels Parish in the summer of 2000 has no ministries that we do not have now. This is an area where the Churches in our country have taken the renewal of Vatican II to heart. It is clear that many ministries are best done by members of the assembly who have the talents and training to do them well.

101

The core of ministry is the assembly: The ministers I imagine at Our Lady of the Angels have been and continue to be exemplary assembly members in their full, conscious and active participation. These people understand what it means to step forward and proclaim a reading, minister Holy Communion, or sing in the choir. Parishes might set a limit on the number of years a person serves in a ministry, asking that each person take off a year after four or five years in a single ministry. This limit would refresh people in their primary role as assembly members.

102

103   The best floor plans manifest the entire assembly as the body enacting this liturgy, so that the ministers come from the assembly rather than sit as a separate group. Many of us remember living with an understanding that the liturgy was simply the work of a priest. Now we have begun to grasp in what way the assembled Church, the Body of Christ, celebrates the liturgy together with the presider. What, then, is the ministry of the ordained priest at Sunday Mass?

104   In our Catholic tradition, the one who is called by the Church to the order of priest is to be in the local parish community as the presence of the bishop. The bishop remains always for us in a direct relationship with every parish of the Diocese. He is also our bond with the Catholic Church through the world and the Church of all the ages. But the bishop, since the early centuries of the Church, has laid hands on other worthy members of the Church and sent them to be his presence with the scattered communities. On Sunday, the one who presides, the ordained priest, comes not only as other ministers do, from the assembly, but comes as

the one who "orders" this assembly, who relates this assembly to the bishop and to the larger Church. True to our Catholic soul, we understand our Church bonds to be more flesh and blood than theory and theology. Here, in this human being, is our bond with the bishop and with the other communities throughout the world and the centuries.

3. Steps you can take

I will be asking priests and others in leadership to begin preparing themselves and the parishes to make much progress by the year 2000 in our Sunday Liturgy. Here are several habits that each churchgoing Catholic can begin to cultivate that will bring us together into a life-giving liturgical practice Sunday after Sunday.

105

• *Become people who worship in the midst of the Sunday Liturgy.* Know which Gospel and New Testament letters we are currently reading on Sundays, and use these for daily reading. Bring to the prayer of intercession on Sunday all that you pray for; take from it persons to be remembered daily by you; when you hear the news of the community and the world, hear it as a Christian who must in prayer lift up the world's needs. Mark with prayer your morning rising and your evening going to bed: the Lord's Prayer certainly, but also some song or psalm from the songs and psalms of Sunday Liturgy in your parish.

106

• *Become people who prepare themselves for Sunday Liturgy and people for whom Sunday Liturgy is preparation for the week.* Seek little ways that can help you make the Lord's Day as much as possible a day when liturgy has room. Find some habit for Sunday morning that helps you anticipate being together as a Church to do the liturgy. Find just one steady practice that makes you stretch toward the Reign of God we glimpse at Mass: It might be a way to make more real the collection that happens on Sunday for the Church and the poor; extending the peace of Christ that you receive each Sunday to others in need of that peace; or fasting from food or distractions and so becoming thoroughly hungry for God's Word and the Eucharistic banquet. In ethnic communities we find many

107

examples of practices that resonate with the Sunday Liturgy, such as the blessing of children that is so much to be praised in Hispanic families.

108 • **At the Liturgy, be the Church.** Know the awesome responsibility you share for making this liturgy! Do not hide; do your private praying in the other hours of the week. Welcome one another, be at peace with one another. Sit together. Sing songs from your heart. Do not be afraid to show in your eager attention that you are hungry for God's Word when the readers read, hungry for Christ's Body and Blood when you come forward in Holy Communion. Give thanks and praise to God by your great attention in the Eucharistic Prayer. Keep your eyes open to one another and do everything you can to build up the Church, the Body of Christ. If the presider or homilist needs help, do not criticize — help.

109 • **Apart from the Liturgy, be the Church.** Remember we are always the Body of Christ, always in communion with one another.

Know that you can ask for help from one another. Let others know that. In the simplest deeds of daily life at work or at home, be conscious of this life we share in Christ, of its joy and its hope. Do not set yourself as separate from others, but understand that we who are the Church are one with others. In us, God is calling and blessing and sanctifying the world God loves. Look at the liturgy as a remote preparation for your week. Listening to God's Word on Sunday morning is preparation for the listening we do for God's Word in our lives all week. The thanks we proclaim at the Eucharistic Prayer is a preparation for thanks over all tables and all meals, and also over all. The common table of Holy Communion is a preparation for looking at the whole world.

- *Give thanks always.* Pray grace at meals even when you are alone in the traditional prayer of "Bless us, O Lord," or a phrase as simple as "Let us give thanks to the Lord our God; it is right to give thanks and praise!" Sing when you are with others at table. If your morning and night prayer is not permeated with praise and thanks to God, enrich it with verses of psalms and prayers from our tradition. (For example, "We worship you, we give you thanks, we praise you for your glory," "Te bendecimos, te adoramos, te glorificamos, te demos gracias por tu santa gloria." Or, "Blessed be God for ever!" "Bendito seas por siempre Señor." Or any or all of Psalm 148.) Cultivate moments of contemplation even during the busiest day, when gratitude can flow from the goodness of a person, any element of creation, or any good work of human making.

110

PART TWO

A MESSAGE TO PRIESTS AND OTHERS WHO HAVE RESPONSIBILITY FOR THE SUNDAY LITURGY

IN GRATITUDE

111 This message is about Eucharist, about the Sunday prayer of praise and thanksgiving. First, then, I give thanks to God for the attention to the liturgy consistently given by priests in this Archdiocese. Without your leadership, on what ground could this Letter stand?

112 Many of you, like myself, were prepared for ministry before Vatican II. What the Council offered us was wonderful, but difficult. Many of us did not readily grasp what the *Constitution on the Sacred Liturgy* asked of us. Those prepared after Vatican II have had to contend with various understandings and approaches to the liturgy. Many of you who work in this Archdiocese were prepared for your ministry in other lands, cultures and languages, and you have had to make many transitions. If I now ask even more of you, I do it with full gratitude.

113 I invite you to share this gratitude of mine with those in the parishes who have worked with you to build up the liturgy of the Church.

114 What follows addresses you as priests, and also addresses the many who join you in taking responsibility for the Sunday Liturgy. Please know that I am myself committed to this work. Together we will approach the Jubilee Year doing what will have the greatest impact on the Church of the next Millennium in our Archdiocese.

I will do all I can to support your efforts to implement this   *115*
Letter over the next years. But as always, the good to be done comes
from all those working at the parish level. Please reflect on what I
am sharing here. I hope you can make it your own because I believe
that the Church in Los Angeles — as magnificent as it is diverse,
with many challenges but with innumerable blessings — can flourish in this renewal.

Leaders Who Need and Embrace the Assembly

I want to be clear: I believe we are at a crucial place in the Church's   *116*
liturgical renewal. We can abandon it, believing that what we have
now is what the renewal intended, or we can learn from the past
— mistakes and successes — and go forward. I want to invite all of
us to go forward together.

We have learned that the renewal of the liturgy cannot take   *117*
on its own course apart from the renewal of catechesis, the building
up of our Churches as places where justice is done, and the
strengthening of our parishes as communities. I do not mean that

liturgy will take sole precedence for several years, and then we will then turn to religious education, then outreach, then community.

118   Rather, we will focus on the liturgy with concrete goals and deadlines for implementation. But I understand that this is how we will learn to do catechesis well and thoroughly for children, for adults, catechumens and the baptized. And I understand that this is how we will become people who see clearly where justice must be done with the liturgy as our constant strength and inspiration for doing this justice. And I understand that building our liturgical practice is the only way we as Catholics make our parishes communities.

119   We must keep all these aspects of being the Church before our eyes in these years. As parish leaders, whatever your own special expertise or interest might be, work together for such strength in the Sunday assembly. Seek and discover how that assembly — and not just the dedicated few — can be about evangelization and catechesis, justice and outreach, the ministering to each other in community. Implementation of this Letter begins and continues when pastor, staff, council and liturgy committee have a firm grasp of the way these aspects of being Catholic are related.

120   The agencies of the Archdiocese and I will support you, but each parish will have to develop its own approach. By the summer of the year 2000, can we all be somewhere near where Our Lady of the Angels is? I think we can because much has already been done. Our achievements in preparing ministers, liturgy committees, and coordinators are outstanding. Build on this success.

121   It will be necessary and helpful to set goals and timetables, to decide on means of presenting good liturgical practice to the parish as a whole, and to critique present practice and be realistic about how it falls short.

122   How do we move from where we are to something more like the intense, nourishing and life-rehearsing Sunday Mass I described in Part One? The most basic answer is that we begin to believe we are an assembly celebrating and being transformed by the liturgy. We begin to believe it and to act that way.

Too often many of us who preside have acted as if it would be enough to hold people's attention, to give them a bit of inspiration, to make them feel better after than before. These are not wrong things to do, but they have little to do with the reality of what liturgy is for Catholics, and little to do with what the Council set as our agenda in paragraph 14 of the *Constitution on the Sacred Liturgy*. We can learn from what we have done so far. We will not have a renewal of the liturgy as long as there remains the habit that some do the liturgy and others attend, some give and some receive, some prepare and others just get there. 123

We need to have in both mind and heart the Council's vision of a Church that can, with strong leadership, achieve the full, conscious and active participation that is the "primary, indeed the indispensable source from which the faithful are to derive the true Christian spirit" (*Constitution on the Sacred Liturgy*, 14). How else can this Church live without that spirit? And where else can such spirit be found? We will receive eagerly our Tradition, celebrate our rites, from Sunday to Sunday and season to season, so that we are slowly fashioned into Catholics whose lives are God's own love for the world. 124

Do not miss what is implicit in paragraph 14: Liturgy is liturgy when it is the habitual deed of the Church. These assemblies must know it deeply and thoroughly, as something so beautiful and profound that repetition only enhances our love for these deeds and our growth from them. Unlike so much else in our modern lives, liturgy is not diversion or entertainment, not measured by any standard suitable to those worlds. It is instead an orchestration of word and silence, chant and gesture, procession and attention, that we are to know, wonderfully, by heart. 125

We must face a primary obstacle head on. After the Council, nowhere did the institutional Church seem to know how to do what the *Constitution on the Sacred Liturgy* saw as absolutely essential for renewal: the condition that the "pastors of souls, in the first place, become fully imbued with the spirit and power of the liturgy and attain competence in it." We cannot go on unless we attend to 126

this foundational element of the renewal. I have no single answer as to how this might be done.

127   My commitment must be to offer to all who are ordained the challenge and opportunities to go deeper into the liturgy, to discover firsthand what the Council's summons is about, and to lead parishes toward renewal. But the goal of this Letter is not the mechanical implementation of what follows. This Letter is a summons to let renewal come from our own disciplined and emerging sense for what is right in liturgy. We cannot survive another generation of external change without deep love of the liturgy and the life we are to find in its celebration.

128   I will speak of the "Qualities of the Presider," "Catechesis for the Liturgy," "Challenges," and "A Schedule of Implementation." The first three summarize the areas where the most work is needed. The fourth attempts to make concrete some basic steps. These basic steps can be offered only because of work already done: by the parishes, the Office for Worship and other agencies of the Archdiocese.

Qualities of the Presider

No single personality type makes a good or poor presider. Some may bring more of the gifts necessary to the task; others may cultivate more strenuously the required disciplines and make up for the gifts they lack. We may not have attended as we might have to the gifts to be sought in a presider or the discipline to become skilled in presiding. I want to emphasize some elements of the presider's task that could most benefit from work in these next years.

129

The presider serves the liturgy that this Church, in all its diversity, is celebrating. Often, we who preside seem not to trust the liturgy. We have all experienced this: the presider who talks too much, or who must prove his humor or piety again and again, or who keeps the other ministers guessing as to what will happen next, or who lets his own way of doing things or his own feelings of the moment dictate. What happens? He has claimed the liturgy as his own and made the assembly an audience. This ends any possibility of a Church enacting its liturgy in this sacred space.

130

Presiders who act in these ways fail to trust both the liturgy and the Church. All presiders need to be within an assembly led by a priest who has achieved the art of trusting the Church to do its liturgy. What a good thing it is when the "audience" mentality has disappeared both in presider and assembly! Although such opportunities may complicate our schedules, we must seek them out. And even when the presiding is less than we might wish, occasionally being in the assembly at Sunday Liturgy builds our desire for a renewed liturgy as little else can.

131

But that is only part of the answer. Until there is a clear sense for how the assembly, served by many good ministers, celebrates the liturgy Sunday by Sunday, presiders may rush into a vacuum and try to fill it. Thus we have to progress in two areas at the same time: in the self-awareness of presiders and in the parish's progress — that is, parishioners responding to God's call, coming Sunday by Sunday in full expectation and need of doing all they must to make good liturgy.

132

133   A presider prepares by knowing thoroughly the flow of the liturgy in this community, which is why it is never ideal when presiders are "circuit riders." They need to know how *this* liturgy is celebrated *Sunday after Sunday* by *this* assembly. The presider must know about timing, the length of silences (after "let us pray," for example), the pace of the procession, what is sung and what is spoken, what the other ministers do, and when and how they do it. The audience/performer feeling sets in as soon as the assembly perceives, usually subconsciously, that this presider will act according to his own notions of pace, what is sung and what is not, silences or lack of them. Then liturgy, as we are trying to understand it, will not be fully celebrated.

134   Preparation to preside is about care with every text to be spoken or sung at a liturgy. This applies certainly to the central tasks of the presider: proclaiming the presidential prayers and the Eucharistic Prayer. But it applies also to the various invitations, greetings and the blessing. And if there are optional "exhortations," then these also need to be prepared. Even those who are gifted with good voices need to grapple with the words before making them part of the Church's liturgy.

135   A good presider is thoroughly attentive to the liturgy, just as every member of the assembly must be. He visibly attends to the readings, joins in the singing, and keeps silent and still when that is expected of everyone else. The presider is "there" for the liturgy, thoroughly engaged in the ritual. This is an attitude, a way of being and conducting oneself. It can happen only when we realize that "presiding" is not merely an item in an ordained person's job description. The presider comes to the liturgy expecting much from the assembly, other ministers and the Lord. He comes with hunger and thirst for God's Word, for making intercession, for giving thanks to God. We ask this of all members of the assembly.

136   The presider does not expect to be carried by emotion or by the good or sad feelings of the moment. The rites of the Church are capable of touching every possible human emotion because they are not dependent on the feelings of the moment. Our rites are

filled with passion, but it is the Church's passion, the deep caring for the world, for creation, for God's love to be manifest. Ritual is, in a good play of words, about the passion of Christ. That leads directly to the next aspect of presiding.

The presider respects symbol. What we do at liturgy takes us beyond the literalness that dominates our lives. To preside, a person must live from the rich ambiguity of symbolic reality.

Respect for the power of symbol does not come easily. Even in the Church, we are afraid of symbol. We want the facts, the dimensions. We want a literal truth, but the literal can never be "the way and the truth and the life." Symbols get beneath the surfaces and are true and real. The symbols we live by are large, ambiguous, and always engaging us anew. One who would preside at liturgy must be practiced in reverence for the symbolic reality of the deeds done by the Church at liturgy. Think how the early preachers in the Church could expound over and over again on a deed like Baptism, knowing it from a dozen sides, scores of Scriptures to be quoted and examined because each gave them some new insight and none exhausted whatever happens in the Baptismal waters. Is that pool of water a womb or a tomb? Is this a marriage bath or a funeral bath or a birth bath? It is all!

The symbolic deed done with power and reverence is fundamental. At Sunday Eucharist, there is reverence for the Body of Christ when we have eaten bread that is bread to all the senses, and when we habitually have enough wine for the cup to be shared by every communicant. Do not deprive these symbols — bread, wine, eating, drinking — of their power. Our more careful planning helps us avoid taking from the tabernacle hosts consecrated at a previous Mass because we have given thanks over *this* bread and wine on *this* altar.

Presiders need to nurture immense respect for our Catholic sense of symbol, of sacrament. We want to know the depth of the things done, used, and said in liturgy, whether this be immersion in water, fragrant anointing with chrism, Word proclaimed from a worthy book of Scriptures, or bread and wine on an altar that is

137

138

139

140

surrounded by Baptized persons giving God praise and thanks in the voice of the presider and in their own voices.

141   More than catechisms or homilies, the symbols, when they are respected and done fully, are the teachers of the Church. But these symbols are not things or abstractions. They are the whole engagement of assembly and its ministers in the deeds that define them. Doing their symbols, Christians form Christians. Those who would take on the role of presider must in these years examine themselves and learn the ways in which they either foster the power of our symbolic actions, or reduce these actions to one-dimensional, impoverished signs.

142   **A presider has a "liturgical piety," a spirit formed and continually formed anew by the liturgy.** This is what the *Constitution on the Sacred Liturgy* calls that "true Christian spirit" that is sought and found in full, conscious and active participation in the liturgy.

143   There are various valid expressions of Catholic piety, but the test of every piety is the liturgy.

144   For example, a priest may know the Bible from a scholarly perspective, but still need to discover how it sounds and what it means when its words are spoken powerfully in the midst of the Church and attended to by an assembly. Liturgical piety and spirituality crave God's spoken Word, pondered in silence and in homily amidst the lives of people and the life of the world. Or a priest may know a variety of theological discussions of what transpires in the Eucharistic Prayer, but may know little of what it looks like, how it sounds, and how passionate the moments can be when the Sunday assembly regularly is engaged in the Eucharistic remembering, acclamation and intercession that is their Eucharistic Prayer, the center of this liturgy, the deed that is shaping their lives. A liturgical piety's essence will be the habit of such praise and thanksgiving. We must avail ourselves of opportunities to experience liturgy celebrated this way.

Catechesis for the Liturgy

When the reforms of the liturgy were introduced after Vatican II, there was often little preparation. However, experience showed that when parishes were well prepared with catechesis in various forms, the reforms were embraced and the liturgy came to be celebrated with care and enthusiasm.   *145*

If we as an Archdiocese are to make serious efforts at renewal these next three years, then catechesis must be a part of this.   *146*

The primary form of catechesis I want to call forth during these three years involves preaching, in part because I want this catechesis to reach every practicing Catholic. But also because I believe it can be done in fidelity to the norms for the homily, and I want us to form a good habit of this kind of preaching.   *147*

For an example of what I mean by a homily that includes catechesis for or about the liturgy, consider the well-known words of Augustine: *148*

If, then, you wish to understand the Body of Christ, listen to the apostle as he says to the faithful, "You are the Body of Christ, and his members" (1 Corinthians 12:27). If, therefore, you are the Body of Christ and his members, your mystery has been placed on the Lord's table, you receive your mystery. You reply "Amen" to that which you are, and by replying you consent. For you hear "The Body of Christ," and you reply "Amen." Be a member of the Body of Christ so that your "Amen" may be true. (Sermon 272)

149   His words could be a contemporary homily on any of those summer Sundays when Mark's Gospel is interrupted for the reading of the sixth chapter of John's Gospel. What does Augustine do here that most of us fail to do even when the opportunities are right before us? To begin, he knows the whole of the liturgy as a source for his preaching. We tend to limit ourselves to the Scripture readings. Augustine has before him the day's Scriptures, its psalms and songs, the season's whole milieu, and the memory of how our assembly celebrates the liturgy. He can summon to his own and the assembly's consciousness the Sunday Eucharist every Sunday, the baptizing every year, the anointing whenever someone is ill. These memories of deeds we have done together are a common language.

150   Augustine can preach that language! How he can preach it! It is a language that the catechumens are slowly beginning to speak, a language that the long-baptized are still learning although now it is not as familiar as their mother tongue. It is a language of gathering around the flames of candles and oil lamps, of tasting milk and honey on the night of Baptism, of hunger and thirst, of touching and tasting the consecrated bread and wine every Lord's Day, of hearing and seeing the waters of the font receive the bodies of the beloved elect and return them newborn in Christ, and of seeing, smelling and reaching out to touch the fragrant oil that flows down the faces of the newly baptized at the great Vigil each year.

151   The reason Augustine and so many others of that time could preach this way is that the rites themselves must have been done with great strength, with respect for symbol and the goodness of

repetition. And even as we strive to celebrate with such participation in our rites, we can preach from what we are already experiencing. I am not talking about inviting the assembly to celebrate any part of the liturgy better. Rather, this kind of catechetical preaching invites the assembly to join with the preacher in reflecting on what has been their experience so far.

For example, it is the experience of the assembly members to say "Amen" when the minister addresses them with these words, "The Body of Christ," "The Blood of Christ." The preacher asks: Ponder what that experience means. Did you hear this or realize that? Do you ever remember these Gospel words of Jesus or these verses of the psalmist? Does it ever overwhelm you how this touch is like the ways human beings touch one another? Perhaps the preacher needs to talk to people and find out what they would think about this communion experience if they were asked to think about it. Perhaps the preacher needs to talk with ministers of Communion to garner their wisdom about their ministry and the community they serve.

This catechesis for the liturgy will probably be difficult for us at first. But we learn the language by doing the deeds. We may discover that many members of the Sunday assembly (perhaps especially those with strong ethnic identity) are ready to speak this language, have been practicing it all their lives, and will welcome it joyfully. But the language must not outrun the reality. If we begin to speak about the many-splendored gesture called the Sign of the Cross, we will need to know how to make that gesture with dignity, reverence and a sense of participation in something ancient. If we begin to speak about the "Amen" we say to the minister's "Body of Christ," "Blood of Christ," we will want to know that the bearing, speech, eyes and posture of the ministers of Communion confirm all that we say.

This preaching from the liturgy does not exhaust the ways of doing catechesis for the liturgy. Here we will need to strengthen the relationship between those who work in liturgy and those who work in catechesis. You whose ministry it is to teach, whether at a graduate level or a pre-school level: Are you not members of the assembly

152

153

154

who celebrate your parish liturgy? And you who prepare liturgy, are you not people formed by your teachers and still being catechized and catechizing others in many ways? These are just two facets of being a Church.

155   I want to encourage all parish ministers to explore possibilities for even fuller collaboration, especially in sacramental preparation. How can the present and emerging forms of liturgical life be the source and subject of catechesis? We need the service of those who have special knowledge in the many areas of parish life, recognizing that all are ritual and sacramental beings whether they teach or are taught, and all are in search of knowledge and meaning when they celebrate their rites. This kind of recognition — that we stand on common ground — will multiply energies and enable everyone to serve a Church in desperate need of learning, formation, and liturgy.

156   These next years are a time to push hard in this direction at every level. Let catechists, teachers and Directors of Religious Education, teachers in our Catholic Schools, see how a strong parish liturgical life forms Christians. And let those who work in liturgy know that the stronger the assembly's participation in the liturgy, the greater the need for all forms of instruction and catechesis. The goal is not aesthetic liturgy or age-appropriate understandings of a catechism. The goal is a Church that is acting on God's love for the world. We must come back, again and again, to Matthew 25: "Amen, I say to you, whatever you did for one of these least brothers or sisters of mine, you did for me."

Challenges

157   **The Homily.** The homily is liturgy. Its words are the words of the liturgy as much as the prayers of the presider or the songs of the assembly. We are told time and again that faithful Catholics want good preaching and homilists who develop and hone their skills.

158   The homilist needs an ear for speech and an eye for the significance of the everyday and the extraordinary. A homilist needs time to delve into all sorts of worlds, to silently ponder and to write. A homilist needs the habits of reading and listening to good

speaking. Even with all that, a homilist needs to speak with conviction within and to the Church.

The approach and guidelines of the U.S. bishops in our 1979   *159*
document, *Fulfilled in Your Hearing,* should be studied and applied.
Take to heart the germ of an idea in that document: that homilists
meet regularly with members of the assembly to read and ponder
the Sunday Scriptures.

The Eucharistic Prayer. What we have often done well for the   *160*
Liturgy of the Word, we must now do for the Liturgy of the
Eucharist. We must engage the Eucharistic Prayer itself, "the center
and summit of the entire celebration" (GIRM: 54). I have spoken
of this above in describing the liturgy at Our Lady of the Angels.

By 2000, let it be obvious to the visitor and let it be deep   *161*
in the heart of the regular churchgoer: When called upon to lift
up our hearts, we do so! And with hearts lifted up to God we all
give God thanks and praise, call upon God's Holy Spirit, remember
God's gracious deeds, intercede once more, and seal all this with

our Amen. The "center and summit" is yet too often the neglected and misunderstood.

162   How can we be ourselves, the Baptized, unless we begin to pray the Eucharistic Prayer fully? How is it chanted or proclaimed? How well do the acclamations acclaim? How is it, even if subtly, set off from the preparation rite and the Communion Rite? How does the very appearance of the sacred altar — the plate of bread that is bread to all the senses, the cup of wine and the flagon full of wine for the whole assembly — center us?

163   This change will require catechesis and preparation of presiders and musicians. Let us begin now. Attend to the bread of life: Let it satisfy the requirements of the *General Instruction*, let it be ample for each Eucharist. Attend to the cup of everlasting life: Let it be there for all at every Sunday Mass. Attend to the text: Those responsible should determine the way that the approved texts for the Eucharistic Prayer will be prayed through the course of the year. The choice of Prayer should not be at the sole discretion of the presider, but should reflect the aspirations and needs of this community. It is the entire assembly's prayer. Attend to the manner of proclamation and acclamation as a first step in making the Prayer a clear center of our Sunday Mass.

164   **The Communion Rite.** Again, although there is much to be done, these tasks are simply implementing the reforms of Vatican II. Now they can be done with some wisdom and good catechesis. The Communion Rite begins with the Lord's Prayer and ends with the Prayer after Communion. It is the work of the assembly and should be treated as such. Let all raise their hands in prayer for the Our Father and through the acclamation "For the kingdom . . ." Let the peace be shared with warm embraces and clasping hands, for here every human relationship of blood or friendship fades before the closeness we have as members of Christ's Body.

165   Then let the litany "Lamb of God" bring attention back to the table where the breaking of bread still speaks of Christ among us, as it did at Emmaus. Let the litany last as long as it takes for the bread to be broken, the cups to be prepared and the ministers to

take their places. Then immediately all are called to the table: "This is the Lamb of God . . ."

There is to be a true procession that makes sense in the con‐figuration of the church. This processing continues throughout the Communion with singing that begins immediately after the accla‐mation, "Lord, I am not worthy . . . " as Communion itself does. Great attention has to be given to the arrangement of ministers and to the flow of the procession around and through the assembly. The songs used at Communion should be ones that all can sing without books in their hands, each parish having perhaps six or seven Communion songs that are able to bear repetition, in word and melody, through the years. This singing of a single Communion song lasts until the procession and all the sharing of Holy Communion end.   *166*

Then the assembly is seated. This is followed by an adequate time of silence, of stillness. On some Sundays the assembly may sing a thanksgiving hymn. And finally, the Prayer after Communion. The announcements, if any, always follow this prayer.   *167*

I must add two additional points. First, the practice of distrib‐uting hosts consecrated at a previous Mass is nowhere envisioned in the Church's liturgy nor in the rubrics. Nor would it be allowed by a right understanding of the Eucharistic Prayer and the assembly. It should be done only when some unusual circumstance has led to too little consecrated bread for the present liturgy.   *168*

Second, receiving both the Body and the Blood of Christ is to be the practice of every parish at every Sunday Liturgy. Homilists should occasionally make reference to the fullness of the symbol that is now extended to every communicant. The words of Jesus are spoken in every Eucharistic Prayer: Take this, all of you, and drink from it. The words are there, inviting the homilist to dwell on them. Those who minister the "cup of everlasting life" should do so with joy and welcome.   *169*

Assemblies That Manifest Our Catholic Soul. A number of chal‐lenges in the celebration of the liturgy might best be understood under this heading.   *170*

171 • The physical make-up of the worship space should go as far as possible to make welcome the handicapped, the elderly, and parents with young children. They too are the Church and welcome us as we welcome them. Cry rooms were a well-meaning but mistaken effort. The liturgy, well celebrated, touches more dimensions than any of us dare name. Beware of liturgy so "adult" that the child is not at home.

172 • Language and culture were mentioned in the Introduction. This is a complex matter, but not as complex as we would sometimes make it. All of us can, as a first step, sing acclamations and litany refrains in other languages. We can above all strive to hold two difficult but correct directions together: our liturgy's openness to the arts of a culture, and our need to bear witness Sunday by Sunday that here in our assemblies all the segregations of society are overturned and there is a common song sung by a great diversity of people.

173 • Horizontal inclusive language, at least to the extent encouraged by the U.S. bishops in their work of revising liturgical books, should be incorporated into all liturgical celebrations of this Archdiocese.

A Schedule for Implementation

174 As we approach the Jubilee Year, and the dedication of this Archdiocese's new Cathedral of Our Lady of the Angels, we dedicate ourselves to a continuing, emphatic renewal of the Sunday Eucharistic Liturgy in our parishes.

175 Out of all that has been said here, I want to single out a number of milestones that can be used through these years. Depending on progress already made, a parish may adapt these, but every parish needs to start now on a course of catechesis and liturgical practice that will bring us to the year 2000 with hundreds of parishes celebrating liturgy more like the one I tried to describe above, even at the cost of delaying other important pastoral initiatives.

1. By Pentecost 1998: responsibility, evaluation and a plan.

Where does responsibility for the liturgy rest? With the pastor, certainly, but who assists him? How effective and helpful are the relationships between principal people? If they need improving, how will this be done? If the parish has no one competent in the work of liturgy coordination, and no group or committee to support it, then finding a liturgy coordinator or committee must come first. In some parishes the formation of this committee, under a trained director, may occupy the better part of a year. In other parishes, it may be that long before anyone can be trained through the Certification Program of the Office for Worship. In some cases, the pastor or someone else on the staff who is trained in liturgy can assume responsibility.

176

There is no one right way to organize the work of preparing the liturgies celebrated in a parish. Each parish will begin from where it is, and as soon as possible establish a plan for liturgical renewal, especially of Sunday Eucharist, by the year 2000.

177

178   **2. By the end of August 1998: a plan for looking carefully at five areas during the fall of 1998.**

179   • Worship space: Does the arrangement, furnishing and beauty of the present worship space help or hinder the full, conscious and active participation of the assembly? Often the limitations of existing buildings must be accepted. But accept them with the imagination to use that space in the best way possible: How can it be used so that neither the presider, ministers nor assembly itself thinks of the assembly as an audience?

180   • Music: First, has it become almost a matter of course that the liturgy is sung and that the music to do this is worthy and bears the repetition by revealing in word and sound ever deeper levels of participation? Second, do the acoustics and sound system provide not only for presider, lector and cantor to be heard by the assembly, but, equally important, for the assembly to hear itself? The sound of the assembly singing should be a primary goal of good acoustics in the church.

181   • Ministries: Assess strengths and weaknesses in the preparation and ongoing training and support within each ministry, both those that are more public (lector, cantor, choir, other musicians, ministers of communion, servers, ushers) and others that are equally important (music director, sacristan, liturgical decorators, writers of intercessions). From this evaluation, plan as needed for recruitment (that is fully representative of all members of the parish), training, in-service work, and sometimes retirement.

182   • Presiding and preaching: Involve the presiders themselves in a plan for evaluation and improvement. Review this Letter carefully for setting local priorities for presiders and preachers. In both areas, continuing help is available from our Office for Worship and the Office of Continuing Formation for Clergy.

183   • Mass schedule: This is always difficult for many reasons. The guidelines given in my last Pastoral Letter on Sunday Eucharist, *The Day on Which We Gather*, are helpful and still apply

in every way. (*The Day on Which We Gather*, Guidelines: #V., A. inclusive)

3. By the First Sunday of Advent 1999, every Sunday Liturgy is celebrated with the Eucharistic Prayer and the Communion Rite as described in this document. Many parishes are ready now to begin this implementation. In others, much work must first be done with the ministries, songs, and overall care given to the liturgy. Here is a summary of (but not a substitute for) what was said above:

• The Eucharistic Prayer is the prayer of the gathered assembly prayed by the presider. It should be clear to all by the intense participation of the assembly that this is the central moment of the Sunday Liturgy.

• The Eucharistic Prayer should have a clear beginning (the preface dialogue set off from what went before) and an ending (the Amen set off from the Lord's Prayer).

• The choice of text should be determined by an overall plan for the parish.

• The acclamations should be strong, as should the presider's proclamation. The flow of thanksgiving and praise, memorial, invocation of the Spirit and intercession should be chanted or spoken with great reverence and attention.

• The tabernacle is to be approached only when some misjudgment of the amount of bread needed has been made. Otherwise it is not used for Communion at Mass.

• The bread is to appear to the senses as bread. (GIRM: 283)

• There should be ample wine for the Communion of the assembly, and all are to be invited wholeheartedly to share from the cup.

• The *orans* posture (standing with hands outstretched, not linked) is appropriate for all at the Lord's Prayer through "For the kingdom . . ."

184

• The Lamb of God is a litany to be sung all through the breaking of the bread and until the presider is ready to say, "This is the Lamb of God . . ."

• The Communion song, a processional song of the assembly, is to begin immediately after the response, "Lord, I am not worthy . . ." and is to continue until all have received Holy Communion.

• The Communion procession is to be a procession in deed as well as name.

• The ministers of Communion, including the presider, are to give great attention to each person coming to Communion.

• An ample period of silence follows the Communion procession.

• Announcements and other community activities follow the Prayer after Communion.

Overall, catechesis is to accompany every effort to renew the liturgy. This is the work not only of pastor and liturgy committee, but of those in catechetical work. Parishes or clusters of parishes should seek out and employ those with degrees in liturgical studies who have a good pastoral sense. These persons would then assist in the implementation of this Letter and the ongoing care of the liturgy.

185

I invite the appropriate offices and departments of the Archdiocesan Catholic Center to come together to discern how all can assist with and collaborate in the important, life-giving, parish-transforming work I have outlined in this Letter.

186

Conclusion

187   Nothing more clearly and wonderfully defines who we are as Catholics as does the celebration of the Eucharist, the Sacrifice of the Mass. We are the Eucharistic Church historically, and the Eucharist has been at the very heart and center of our beliefs and practices. The Eucharist has sustained persecuted Catholic Communities down through the centuries, even in our own time. Heroic efforts have been taken to celebrate the Eucharist clandestinely in areas of persecution and opposition, thus sustaining the life of the Catholic Church.

188   It is my prayer and hope that the full celebration of the Eucharist at each Sunday Mass across the Archdiocese of Los Angeles will inspire all of our Catholic people to understand ever more fully the precious gift that is ours in this mystery of faith. The full and proper celebration of the Eucharist becomes a powerful teacher for all of us, and the reverence, joy, participation, and silence of our celebrations deepens all of us in the life of Jesus Christ.

189   It was surely above all on "the first day of the week," Sunday, the day of Jesus' Resurrection, that the early Christians met "to break bread" (Acts 20:7). From those early days down to our own time in the Archdiocese of Los Angeles, the celebration of the Eucharist has been continued, so that today we encounter it everywhere in the Church with the same fundamental structure. It remains the very center of the Church's life.

190   Thus, from Eucharistic celebration to Eucharistic celebration, as they proclaim the Paschal Mystery of Jesus "until he comes," the pilgrim People of God advances, "following the narrow way of the cross" (1 Corinthians 11:26), toward the heavenly banquet when all the elect will be seated at the table of the Kingdom forever! [4]

NOTES

1. The topic of the Eucharist is inexhaustible in its many graces and 191
understandings. Like a precious diamond, each view of it offers new
and deeper insights. For the purposes of this Pastoral Letter I wish to
incorporate totally the full teaching of the Church on the Eucharist
as found in the *Catechism of the Catholic Church*, paragraphs 1066 to
1209, on Liturgy, and 1322 to 1419, on the Eucharist. While my
focus in this Letter is on the Sunday celebration of the Eucharist, all
of the teachings and understandings of the Catechism are understood as the principles upon which this Letter stands.

    Given the misunderstanding that sadly exists among some 192
Catholics about the very nature of the Eucharist, I wish to include
paragraph 1376 from the Catechism as a foundational teaching
for all:

> The Council of Trent summarizes the Catholic faith by declaring:
> "Because Christ our Redeemer said that it was truly his body
> that he was offering under the species of bread, it has always been
> the conviction of the Church of God, and this holy Council now
> declares again, that by the consecration of the bread and wine there
> takes place a change of the whole substance of the bread into the
> substance of the body of Christ our Lord and of the whole substance
> of the wine into the substance of his blood. This change the holy
> Catholic Church has fittingly and properly called transubstantiation."

2. Note that the Catechism speaks of the Assembly as one of the 193
very names for the Eucharist: "The Eucharistic assembly *(synaxis)*,
because the Eucharist is celebrated amid the assembly of the faithful, the visible expression of the Church." (1329)

    Pope John Paul II addressed a group of French bishops on 194
March 8, 1997, emphasizing the role of the assembly: ". . . the first

sign is that of the assembly itself. . . . Everyone's attitude counts, for the liturgical assembly is the first image the church gives."

195   3. The *General Instruction of the Roman Missal* states:

> Following the example of Christ, the Church has always used bread and wine with water to celebrate the Lord's Supper. (281)

> According to the tradition of the Church, the bread must be made from wheat; according to the tradition of the Latin Church, it must be unleavened. (282)

> The nature of the sign demands that the material for the eucharistic celebration appear as actual food. The eucharistic bread, even though unleavened and traditional in form, should therefore be made in such a way that the priest can break it and distribute the parts to at least some of the faithful. (283)

196   Consequently, parishes are strongly urged to use bread for the Eucharist that more closely resembles bread. Recipes for approved altar breads are available from our Office for Worship.

197   4. See the Catechism, especially paragraphs 1337 through 1344.